VIOLIN PLAY-ALONG

AUDIO ACCESS INCLUDED

GEORGE GERSHWIN

PLAYBACK+
Speed • Pitch • Balance • Loop

To access audio visit:
www.halleonard.com/mylibrary

Enter Code
3176-6184-3332-9070

Cover photo is from the George Grantham Bain collection at the Library of Congress.

ISBN 978-1-4950-6284-1

7777 W. BLUEMOUND RD. P.O. BOX 13819 MILWAUKEE, WI 53213

In Australia Contact:
Hal Leonard Australia Pty. Ltd.
4 Lentara Court
Cheltenham, Victoria, 3192 Australia
Email: ausadmin@halleonard.com.au

Visit Hal Leonard Online at
www.halleonard.com

Jon Vriesacker, violin

Audio arrangements by Peter Deneff

Recorded and Produced by Jake Johnson at Paradyme Productions

Embraceable You

from CRAZY FOR YOU

Music and Lyrics by George Gershwin and Ira Gershwin

I Got Rhythm

from AN AMERICAN IN PARIS

Music and Lyrics by George Gershwin and Ira Gershwin

Love Is Here to Stay

from GOLDWYN FOLLIES

Music and Lyrics by George Gershwin and Ira Gershwin

The Man I Love

from LADY BE GOOD

Music and Lyrics by George Gershwin and Ira Gershwin

Prelude II

Andante con moto e poco rubato from *3 Preludes*
By George Gershwin

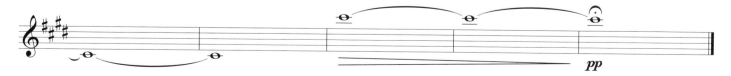

Rhapsody in Blue

By George Gershwin

* cue notes optional

They Can't Take That Away from Me

from THE BARKLEYS OF BROADWAY

Music and Lyrics by George Gershwin and Ira Gershwin

Summertime

from PORGY AND BESS ®

Music and Lyrics by George Gershwin, DuBose and Dorothy Heyward and Ira Gershwin